HOUSEHOLD INVENTORY

HOUSEHOLD INVENTORY

Poems by Connie Jordan Green

BRICK ROAD
POETRY PRESS

Cover photo credit: *Alcatraz* © Keith W. Badowski
Author photo credit: Phyllis Price

Library of Congress Control Number: 2015932313
ISBN-13: 978-0-9898724-3-0

Published by Brick Road Poetry Press
P. O. Box 751
Columbus, GA 31902-0751
www.brickroadpoetrypress.com

Brick Road logo by Dwight New

To my family and to my writing friends
and mentors—you are all a blessing.

Acknowledgments

Grateful acknowledgment is made to the editors of the following journals and anthologies in which the poems listed were published the first time, sometimes in a slightly different form:

Anthology of Appalachian Writers, Vol.v: "Making Biscuits" and "She Thinks on Hunger"

Anthology of Appalachian Writers, Vol.vi: "Boy after his Bath" and "No Country for Old Women"

Appalachian Heritage: "Household Inventory"

Bluestone Review: "May" and "Pain"

Cumberland River Review: "Summer Solstice"

drafthorse: "My Father's Gods," "Song to My Husband," and "Tending the Garden"

Fluent: "Into the Meadow" and "Oak Ridge, Tennessee, 1944"

Iowa Woman: "Blackberry Time"

The Kerf: "Ode to an Onion"

Literary Lunch: "Persephone Addresses the Herbs"

Low Explosions: "She Pays Attention" (published as "Paying Attention")

Magnolia, Vol. ii: "Speak These Words"

Main Street Rag: "Reedsong"

Maypop: "Everyday Poem," "The Graveyard School of Tennessee Poets," "How to Spend a February Day," and "Sledging the Poem"

Motif, Vol. 3: "Traveling"

The Notebook (Grassroots Women Project): "Family Lore"

Now & Then: "Soil Test"

Outscape: "From the Pulpit: For the Minister at My Memorial Service"

Poem: "The Goldfish"

Potomac Review: "Winter Rides the Mountains"

Some Say Tomato: "All Tomatoes" and "Maybe, Tomatoes"

Southern Poetry Anthology, Vol.iii: "Boss" and "Late January Letter to a Retired Friend in Florida"

Southern Poetry Anthology, Vol.vi: "Pale Shadow" and "Saturday Matinee"

Sow's Ear Poetry Review: "Evolution"

STILL: The Journal: "Cicadas," "November Moves In," "Poppies," and "Ten Ways of Looking at an Appalachian Woman"

A Tapestry of Voices: "Living with Snakes," "Pastoral," and "Song of the Farmer"

A Tennessee Landscape, People, and Places: "Leaving Eden"

Town Creek Poetry: "Fungus"

Voices from the Valley: "To Robert Frost"

Wavelength: "Gardening"

"Maybe, Tomatoes" was reprinted in *Poem in Your Pocket for Young Poets*.

CONTENTS

Ten Ways of Looking at an Appalachian Woman   /   3

I. SOIL TEST

Persephone Addresses the Herbs   /   7
Tending the Garden   /   8
Ode to an Onion   /   9
Pale Shadow   /   10
To Robert Frost   /   11
No Country for Old Women   /   12
At the Feed Store   /   13
Soil Test   /   14
Ode to the Potato   /   15
Summer Solstice   /   16
Pay Attention   /   17
All Tomatoes   /   18
Maybe, Tomatoes   /   19
Blackberry Time   /   20
Song of the Farmer   /   21
Fungus   /   22
Forgotten   /   23
Cicadas   /   24
November Again   /   25
Leaving Eden   /   26
Gardening   /   27

II. HOUSEHOLD INVENTORY

The Graveyard School of Tennessee Poets   /   31
Oak Ridge, Tennessee, 1944   /   32
Evolution   /   33
Living with Snakes   /   34
Boss   /   35
Decoration Day   /   36
Family Lore   /   37
What If   /   38
Silent Syllables   /   39

Tarmac / 40
Alzheimer's / 41
Saturday Matinee / 42
Household Inventory / 43
Pastoral / 44
Into the Meadow / 45
My Father's Gods / 46
Little Poem for a Small Word / 47
The Goldfish / 48
The Gift / 49
Boy After His Bath / 50
Making Biscuits / 51
Song to My Husband / 52
One More Day / 53
Killing Time / 54

III. TRAVELING COMPANIONS

Sledging the Poem / 57
Symmetry / 58
The Starry Messenger / 59
Everyday Poem / 60
Three Hallelujahs / 61
Praise / 62
What Is The Soul? / 63
Traveling / 64
Mindy at Dusk, 1919 / 65
From a Car Window, June Afternoon / 66
She Thinks on Hunger / 67
She Pays Attention / 68
Speak These Words / 69
Reedsong / 70
On the Wing / 71
November Moves In / 72
Late January Letter to a Retired Friend in Florida / 73
How to Spend a February Day / 74
Pain / 75
Old Age / 76
Poppies / 77
Traveling Companions / 78

Spite   /   80
Winter Rides the Mountains   /   81
From the Pulpit: For the Minister at My Memorial Service   /   82
May   /   83
Self-Portrait   /   84

Ten Ways of Looking at an Appalachian Woman

i.
Among ten tall mountains
the most enduring being is a woman.

ii.
When the stars were flung across the galaxy
the first cells foretold her appearance.

iii.
She is known for her ability to create supper
from a handful of meal and a piece of fatback.

iv.
Veins of coal are nothing
compared to iron in her arteries.

v.
Words are pebbles in her mouth.
She spits them into stone walls.

vi.
Her silence is like a scolding.

vii.
Before dark she does
the work of many men.

viii.
I know not which is most beautiful—
the grace of her body when she is young
or her will when she matures.

ix.
A man and a woman are one,
but a man and a mountain woman
are like the girding of a steel structure.

x.
When she comes at last to rest,
even the ravens fold up their glossy wings.

I. SOIL TEST

Persephone Addresses the Herbs

In the fourteenth and fifteenth centuries ... the harvesting of herbs and vegetables was often accompanied by the chanting of verses or the muttering of spells.

—from *Betty Crocker's Kitchen Gardens*

Lovage, chervil, sweet marjoram,
what has it cost you to remain
safe from winter's wrath
in your airtight jars?
Colors faded, leaves dry as old skin,
still you punctuate our dinner,
give back summer's flavor,
essence of meals almost forgotten.
You awaken memory of sun's long journey.

Here in underground's Stygian gloom
let us praise perennials—mint, sage,
rosemary, tarragon, thyme—hearty
souls who outlast snow, ice,
who endure while our eyes close
on dreams of pale lavender blooms,
gaiety of chamomile flowers.
Blessings upon generous biennials—
angelica, frilly parsley—who hallow
our planting with a second year of growth.

Soon spring and tender basil, sweet
bay, garden cress. May our spirits
rise like green tips of chives
long held prisoner in eternal night.

Tending the Garden

You don't have to know what feeds the seed,
urges its metamorphosis into tendril and stem,

into leaf, flower, fruit, and then seed once more.
You don't have to understand soil, mix of loam

and sand, peat and manure, acidity, alkalinity,
how clay can harden or sponge up moisture,

the role of earthworms tunneling
their evolutionary trails, eating the earth,

casting their wealth. You don't have to measure
rainfall, track sun's northward journey,

its turning at last back toward equinox.
You don't have to learn Latinate nomenclature,

study genetics, Mendel's years of pea vines.
You need only tie on a hat, slip your feet

into last year's sneakers, kneel where sun
and rain, where seasons and weather bless

your bent back, pronounce a beneficence
on your garden-loving soul.

Ode to an Onion

These tears fall for you
  renegade of earth
    pungent parcel
      flavor for soup, meat, and sauce.

Beneath the knife's blade
  your layers part—
    translucent slivers
      crescent moons.

Only the tomato
  rosy in her skin
    juiced without remorse
      rivals your versatility—

in a melodrama, you win
your soul too sweet for tragedy.

Pale Shadow

I pull weeds from bean rows while seeds
that spawned these stalks slumber
among a thousand kin. They will sprout,
the professor of agriculture told me,

for eighty or ninety years yet, their lives
a Methuselah legend my back
will never conquer, like starlight long
dead still traveling its eleven-million miles

per minute, messages our minds will puzzle over
until our own cells and senses blur and dim.
Knees in the dirt, hands searching and tugging,
I bring a temporary order—the same blow

for orderliness I've struck these seventy
years—dishes washed and stacked on shelves,
dirt swept beyond the doorway, sheets
washed, sun-dried, tucked over mattresses—

as if the world wants to be made
perfect, as if the living must print
their pattern, cast a lengthening
shadow before the face of chaos.

To Robert Frost

Often in the spring
I walk my own
steep-pitched pastures
far from Vermont hills.

Old poet, I want to say,
did you, too, love the land
more than words
so that all those lines—

those metered rhymed cadences
that seemed to pour forth
spontaneous as buds
on your beloved birches—

were of less use to you
than plows turning
the good black earth?

No Country for Old Women

This is no country for old women—
cedar waxwings line up
on apple tree limb, pass
petals from beak to beak,
the last fed first, wrens
fledge from their garden shoe
nest near the back door,
cling to porch screen
while mature birds scold
from maple bough.

This is no country for old women—
bucks roam the field,
antlers of velvet polished
against oak and hickory,
does hide spotted fawns
in last fall's leaves, young
deer chase each other
near our garden, surprised
to see our gray heads close
together, bent over the first
mum flowering in late August.

This is no country for old women—
ghosts of children flit
through the house, hide
beneath stairs, in attic rooms,
refuse their vegetables, advice
about their hair, their clothes,
choice of friends. I find their crumbs,
trails they've left, daring me to follow
into a country where old and young
rise together, hands linked
in a chain hauling up memory
like water from a deep well.

At the Feed Store

Bins brim with onion bulbs—
small, covered in crinkly paper
like pages of a family Bible.
Outside, April sky spreads
her blue coverlet over a landscape
of yellow jonquils, tulips, red and pink.
In the shop, we are concerned
with the dormant—bags of shriveled
peas, boxes of potatoes smelling
of earth—only pictures to promise
the green, the luxuriant.

                    I rummage
among the onions, scoop out
a handful, weigh them on a scale
old as the store's oiled floor boards,
dump them into a brown paper bag
I'll carry home, set beside me
while I kneel on the warm black
soil, trowel a hole, bury the bulb,
tip pointing up for growth
straight toward the sun—
like my father before me, tending
the useless that it may
grow into its abundance.

Soil Test

Clear off a patch, any size,
say thirty by forty. Till the soil,
but not deep enough to hit deadpan,
bones of ancient ancestors. Scratch
furrows with your hoe, scarcely disturb
earth for carrots, lettuce, spinach—
seeds small as memory lost to humus.
Cut straight rows for beans, corn,
the sturdy who all summer march across
your garden, a line of teachers, parents
to bend in summer storms but never break.

On a cold March day, set out
broccoli, cabbage, their souls hardened
to spring freezes, winter's last snow.
Bide your time with tomatoes
though warm days will tempt like longings
of your youth—the too-easy kiss,
the car's backseat. In full season,
plant tomato vines, holes deep
to swallow stems, a few leaves
above ground, roots growing their secret
tendrils in June's heat.

As for squash, go in fear, one vine
creeping toward your ordered rows, a rogue
dictator over-running neighbor countries.
Pick male squash blossoms, leaving one
to fertilize the yellow females where bees
pillage and plunder through long summer days.
And the soil itself, replenish
with composted leaves, stems, too-ripe fruits,
manure from cows, chickens, sheep—
earth's remains treasures you'll seek,
your life spent amending, amending.

Ode to the Potato

Oh, hidden one—
eyes that see nothing,
earthworms for companions,
you live your secret life,
multiply your kin
so our shovels spade up
whole families—round,
knobby, elongated, you care
not for appearances, give up
your fleshy bodies for dicing,
mashing, baking, frying,
have saved nations
by your abundance,
have sent millions into famine
when you ail. Oh, apple
of the earth, bless our daily
hunger, our appetite that will
not leave you in peace.

Summer Solstice

after Arthur Smith

For one day we believe
in the high arc of the sun's
journey, how earth tilts
and turns, gifts her halves
with heat, one after another,
days rolling into months
into a new season, how
we stand here and know,
how beneath our feet
burrowed deep, the denizens
of earth's rich dark
tunnel their lives, and above
the wind whispers
through willow oak and shagbark
hickory, how this world whirrs,
its music always overture.

Pay Attention

Corn stalks stretch
   with each rain, leaves
      like funnels pour
         moisture into their hearts.

Tomatoes hide
   behind vines you neglected
      to sucker, blush
         pink, then red, their bursting

presence today's surprise.
   Beans camouflage
      themselves beneath leaves
         in overcrowded rows.

Squash crawls
   at your feet, makes
      its way around sunflower
         and cleome—volunteer

sirens enticing bees,
   hummingbirds, yellow
      finches. Along the fence,
         autumn clematis harbors

mockingbird's nest,
   her scolds pierce
      the July day, your hat
         deflects her dives.

All Tomatoes

Unlike potatoes they have
no need for eyes
growing as they do
in the eye of God

their chief threat
the caterpillar
lumping its way
along the vine

the bird
overhead
eyeing the first
rosy blush.

In their kingdom
after planting
come sun, water, growth
then the ritual

of teeth, tongue, taste—
the yearly spilling
of juices
their sacrificial gift.

Maybe, Tomatoes

if the vines mature
if the caterpillars don't get them

if we water, sucker, feed
if we pick and preserve

maybe, tomatoes
    thin sliced on sandwiches
    chunked into salads
        peeled and whole
        juiced and sauced
            stewed
                pickled
                    stuffed

Blackberry Time

Each July
we belt buckets
around our waists
freeing hands
to pick the berries,
fingers gentle
on the blackest
knowing how easily
juice spills.

First there's a plunk
for each berry
in the bucket,
a sign
the harvest has begun,
then quiet
as the berries
pile into heaps
we'll eat—
juice staining
teeth, tongues,

life slipping
down our throats
the way these berries,
these purple-black
fruits pulled from briars,
slip yearly
between our fingers.

Song of the Farmer

Late September, season's last cutting,
hay falls behind the mower
like pale sheets billowed over a bed.
Dry weather crisps the grass
so baler can do its work—
cut, pack, tie square packages
we load onto a wagon, haul
to barn loft where we build
a fort against winter's hunger.

Come January's cold, we'll feed
the stock—horses huddled
in barn's lee, cows on a hillside,
faces toward the weather—
scatter the gold we collect
this day, remember sun's
warm hand, smell of dryness,
remember how it feels
to have too much.

Fungus

A neighbor to lichen, but soft as a mushroom, grown from nothingness, from earth's will, colors striated—cream to rust to tan to darker brown, lines of green and a hint of orange, the Grand Canyon in microcosm, edged with waves that ruffle like old lace, tea-stained trim on grandmother's dress, a creek over mossy rocks. It smells of earth, the garden's first turning, earthworms tunneling, humus at the bottom of an old bucket, bare toes poking a rotted log. It offers itself in layers, small gatherings above one long ridge. Along its back it has clung to a fallen limb, declared itself soul of the dying tree, negated the heft and weight of forest. It will shelter beetles, will feed browsing deer, their hunger next winter like our need to see again and again, our longing to go deep.

Forgotten

I meant to plant sweet peas
beside the garden fence,
in early May drop the shriveled
seeds so by July vines would climb
the boards, clamber like eager
children over the railing, droop
clusters of blooms for bees, butterflies,
my hungry eyes. Last February
I intended to cut back the muscadine,
prune wild growth that escapes
the arbor, twists tendrils
along redbud limbs, a gang
of teenagers out for a joy ride.
I meant to divide the daylilies,
cut away rotted iris rhizomes,
find a bed for the healthy surplus,
to clean out the potting shed,
organize the rack of garden tools
like old bones entombed in their dark
corner. Daily the sun shrinks its arc
across the sky, blackbirds clatter
from the oak, and even buzzards
have winged toward warmer climates.
I grow old with the year, my good
intentions stretching like a road
whose pebbled surface my feet know
only too well. I have seen where
this trail leads.

Cicadas

Like armored warriors
they signal one another,
sawing out a song
through the sticky day,
their new-found skin
green and black,
slick-looking and strange.
They hang their armor
on tree trunks, claws
grip bark, an empty shell
remembering what it was like
to pulse with life.
Eyes on stilts, they sing
for a mate, their days
above ground more brief
than Persephone's,
the long sleep
a small death they have
escaped, earth a tomb
they can never forget.

November Again

By my front window, two maples
bare their limbs to the wind. Two
other maples remain mostly green,
only their tips like candles ignited
by the sun. I want to hold the season,
a wayward child I know will have
his own way. In another week,
the garden will stand desolate, okra
stalks a monument to lost hope, tomato
vines withered on the fence where
they climbed and glowed a few weeks
ago. Even the birds have abandoned
their bright ways, summer's goldfinch
gone, and now a drab sparrow spears
summer's last seeds. I want to find
joy in change, to build a house of fallen
leaves, to burrow in the dry
odor of all that was once alive,
to know the mutability of season
into season, and be glad.

Leaving Eden

Perhaps it happened
in September, here—

the two figures,
backs to the green garden,
stumbling over rocks—

the hillsides
suddenly wounded
with the bruised hues of fall—

the two awake for the first time
to the fierce beauty of decay.

Gardening

for Dana

It is harvest you say
that sends you through May's planting,
the pleasure to be counted at the end—
jars of beans in a row
like wealth wrested from black soil.

Not so for me, in May harvest
more distant than mountain ranges,
less certain than summer rains.
It is the planting itself—
earth warm from April sun,
rich with winter's leavings;
worms wiggling through spaded
clumps I turn as others turn
pages of their holy book,
my story written in soil
tempered with humus.

Even knowing no harvest
on May mornings I plant—
plant for the joy of digging,
the wonder of work,
promise of seeds,
mystery of soil,
of sun and earth's turning.

II. HOUSEHOLD INVENTORY

The Graveyard School of Tennessee Poets

he names us, as bodies and blood
flow from each pen, tombstones
and eulogies sit beside each elbow,
and death holds us in his bony
grip the way love clutched us
years before in the rage of hormones
and youth, our heads this day
bowed to our papers, requiem
ringing from every legal pad.

Oak Ridge, Tennessee, 1944

Of course there was the boardwalk
the skates sang to, how we dropped
coins through its cracks, milk
money vanishing before we reached
school, and at night, pines
in the wind, a whispering choir
beyond our bedroom window,
oaks towering, their rocky
understory becoming our rooms,
our paths, and far below the house
a gully cutting through clay banks,
warren of imagined animals ready
to pounce, fear an emotion
we had to invent in our daily games—
the cold war and Nikita Khrushchev,
bomb shelters and evacuation routes,
images waiting to haunt
our adolescence,
the simplicity of childhood
a jewel we would turn this way
and that, marvel at the light
bouncing from its many-faceted surface.

Evolution

First she studied mathematics,
the rhythm of sine and cosine,
tangent and cotangent, the pattern
of quadratic equations, reliable
as phases of the moon, the way
numbers and letters mesh, gears
greased by Pythagoras, Archimedes—
music, like breath, bound by measure,
the count of a chant. She was in love
with order, creation ruled by inviolate
principle, an incantation against
wildness beyond her door.

Next, physics, problems of power
and motion in mathematical increments,
the world subject to analysis, Euclid's
axioms branching like the tree
beyond her window, dark against
the winter sky. Biology and botany,
where life beat at cell walls, vibrated
with numbers—Mendel's law,
the recapitulation theory,
creation captured in a formula.

Then her cells began inventing
mathematics—egg and sperm together,
one plus one remaining one,
division become multiplication,
profusion beyond counting.
She turned from columns of numbers,
found words that slid off pages,
spilled so fast her hands couldn't cup
them, a stream that carried her
beyond walls into the garden where vines,
shrubs, trees greeted her, branching
like the blood pulsing in her veins.

Living with Snakes

My mother had nightmares about them,
couldn't look at a picture
of the great coiled body, tongue
like a finger beckoning. She told
how when she was young a neighbor boy
threw a dead snake on her, smooth body
wrapping her neck until she felt its spirit cut
her breath, fear drawing the constrictor close.

My dad kept one in his garden,
long, slender, black, quiet
beneath squash leaves, slipping
across his feet when he bent
to stroke it. Catcher of mice,
moles, whatever would eat
his crops before we could—*leave
it alone*, he told us girls.

I have come to need them,
watch them in the woodpile
where chipmunks spend the summer,
spot one on the basement stairs,
shut the door against my husband's discovery,
dark secret for my eyes only.

Boss

My dead grandfather roams the farmhouse rooms,
peeks into an upstairs chamber
where his own father's handmade cherry casket
sat twenty-four years awaiting the old man's death,
pauses at the door to the front bedroom
he and my grandmother shared.
He wanders into the kitchen,
looks out at the chicken yard,
notes grape vines on the porch posts
grown large as his forearm.
He tastes again breakfasts after milking,
cream from his cows, eggs and ham—
food he grew with the strength
of his body. He sees an old man
at the table, jar of peanut butter
for dinner, his own ghostly presence
after my grandmother's death.
He smells wooden furniture rubbed with beeswax,
linens fresh from the clothesline,
the scent of lilac—early May's gift to the hall table.
He will not go to the barn, will not toss down
from the loft forkfuls of hay that lured
cows to the milking stanchions,
will not go to the garage,
crank his old truck, odor of oil and gasoline
embedded in floor boards.
He roams the house of his parents,
his children, his grandchildren,
visits them all where in life
he had no time to linger.

Decoration Day

Bones called us back to Kentucky.
Year after year we joined our grandmother,
aunts, uncles, cousins, climbed the steep hill

to tombstones leaning against gravity's pull,
stubbornness of those lying there urging
the stones to hold their ground. At the foot
of each grave, the women set vases

of cosmos with their white, pink, maroon
petals, red rambling roses calmed
into an arrangement. The men cut back
briers encroaching on graveyard borders,

trimmed boxwoods set at the family plot.
We children wandered among the graves,
chanted dates and names—*Ida Elizabeth Hall,
born 1911, died 1912, Nellie Marie Hall,*

born and died 1921—our mother's
family less than a memory, known
to us only through story. Overhead
crows circled, settled into the tallest

buckeyes, ruffled their black coats
and cawed a funereal song. A distant
train heading up the steep slope
out of the hollow blew one long

whistle. Around us the dead waited,
sinew and muscle gone to time.

Family Lore

My mother swore he was already engaged
when they met, *to a little red-haired girl*
there in Pulaski, somebody with a pedigree
to match his, she would tell us. Daddy
never said a word, went on spooning
gravy over his mashed potatoes. *He*
didn't tell his family about me until we
were married, knew Janie—my sweet
grandmother who bought us Bobbsey
Twins books, took us into town when
we visited to get our straggly locks shorn—
would put a stop to it.

                Now, Ruth,
Daddy would finally say, *you know*
Mom loves you.

              Mother paid him no
mind. *The truth is*, she said, *his people*
came over on the Mayflower and my people
went out to meet them.

              We three girls
never imagined the blood of gentry
in our veins, knew we, like Mother,
sprang from soil blackened by coal dust,
sprouted where mountains funneled
sunlight to a narrow hollow, could not
imagine open sea, sails unfurling,
vastness of ocean, the dot of a single ship.

What If

What if rain washed the sky to clearest blue,
the smoking slag blossomed with dandelions
and Queen Anne's Lace, the slanted porches,
shaky stairs knit themselves into lumber
fresh from the mill, the smell of resin perfuming the air.

What if the faces of the children rounded
like river rocks, their limbs dimpled like a Renoir.
What if hunger rose like a whirlwind,
shook the leaves along the mountain
as it passed beyond, the miners' lungs
washed themselves white as an altar cloth,
the only bent back that one praying in praise,
their arms scooping not coal but children,
lifting them to the light.

Silent Syllables

Where have the parents of my youth
traveled to in their silent syllables?

—Pablo Neruda

And why were they often silent?
Mother who loved a crowd, cracked wise,
danced with all the men, told jokes,
recounted stories, knew hardship
for what it was—a nut to be beaten
open, kernels picked and chewed
for their bitter fruit.

Daddy whose ancestors settled
the land, built brick houses, planted
rows of boxwood to lead strangers
to the door, silent people whose
mornings and evenings were given
to milking, days to planting, harvesting,
tending, who worked without comment
until they fell dead.

Mother silent only after anger
spent itself with hurled dishes,
scissored photographs, the silence
stretching days, Daddy quietly helping
my sisters and me wash dishes, do
homework, and fall into bed.

Where have they gone, those syllables
of love silently spent in that house
where heat and cold permeated the walls,
seeped into our skin?

Tarmac

I think about Mother there
where smoke rises from the airplane's motor,
the attendant by the emergency door
implores the sightseers,
Slide, then run away from the plane.
My mother's fear as she steps
onto the wing then begins the quick
descent, her heel the first
contact with tarmac. Bones
shatter like a cut-glass bowl
brought too close to fire.

I think about her in the hospital,
foot encased while bones begin
their long reknitting, her friend
waits to bring her back to the states.
Weeks later the plane,
the roar of its motor louder
than her own blood's thrumming.
Then months in a wheelchair
while planes flame in her dreams,
bodies drift down like ash.

I think of her life handed back,
the future stretching before her—
great grandchildren to be born,
her friend's death, her own bones
that will break one by one, brain cells
tangle until memory becomes the present,
the present lost forever, the slide
from the plane again and again
while smoke billows about her head,
her hair fingers of flame
rising toward heaven.

Alzheimer's

With dark come the ghosts,
the awful longing to join them,
be again ten years old, Mother
and Father, sisters, brothers,
all under one roof, separation
an unknown language, death
the babies in the cemetery on the hill.

Not yet the years of moving out,
moving on, lungs filling with coal
dust, kidneys failing, accident
and age dividing what was once whole.
Not yet her husband's sudden
death, her daughters in their separate
homes. Impossible to remember
grandchildren, to know the woman
in the mirror, hair white, back stooped.

Better the ghosts of want and need
closed up in that house, the place
she goes each evening, shadows
like a shawl around her shoulders,
night a blanket she pulls close,
memory a dark room where she knows
all the furniture, can walk about unharmed.

Saturday Matinee

Even in hard times, Mother and Daddy
found fifteen cents for each of us
on Saturday afternoons—nine cents
for the movie, a nickel for Milk Duds
or popcorn or saved for afterwards,
a book of paper dolls at the dime store.

My sisters and I sat through shoot-outs
along dry gulches, stagecoaches
overtaken by men with bandanas
tied over their faces, horses
pounding up clouds of dust, our world
flickering pictures in black-and-white.

All evening Mother hummed
while cooking supper, Daddy patted
her bottom each time he passed near,
we three girls with our heads full
of afternoon movies—Paula Peril
tied to the railroad track, train
whistling around the bend, her fate
awaiting next Saturday, our lives roaring
down the tracks, obstacles unimagined,
Mother and Daddy still hand-in-hand.

Household Inventory

The secretary that belonged to my grandmother—
golden oak I've rubbed over the years—
where she kept the dairy-farm books,
wrote occasional letters to her two sons
who left the farm. The secretary my dad
chose after her death and that my mother
kept as the last real furniture to go with her
into the retirement home and that I chose
when Mother went into the nursing home—
desk surface split along the joint
of two large boards—our friend the wood carver
reglued, reattached—cubby holes now filled
with seed catalogs, public television newsletters,
drawers of bank statements, my father's
gardening journal, deed to my parents' farm,
the last canceled checks from the nursing home.
Now my children eye the household items,
rearrange in their minds the rooms
of their own houses—where to put the secretary
and who will take it—or the corner cupboard,
oak side table from my husband's grandparents,
cedar chest that belonged to my aunt,
confiscated by my mother for an unpaid debt—
all of us debtors, household items
currency we'll pay over and over.

Pastoral

My dad and the bull stand side by side,
pasture fence stretched tight, garage
in the background where my grandfather
parked his Ford truck, staircase rising
to attic storage, dust motes in afternoon
sun, pungent smell of oily rags, crankcase
fluids. My dad is sixteen or seventeen,
slight body beginning to muscle out
to the shape he'll carry into adulthood.
In the photo, the bull is docile,
as all animals were around my dad, could
be the family dog waiting to have his ears
scratched. This is the bull of family stories,
raised on a bottle, groomed and petted,
recipient of blue ribbons at county fairs,
my dad the only one who could step
into a pasture with him, money from his sale
sending Daddy to Virginia Polytechnic Institute
for a dreamed-of year before banks failed,
the country shut down, he went off
to the mining camps, a second chapter written
with marriage, family, labor so different
from the first. His daughters gaze in wonder
at the picture, only his crooked smile to say
this was once my life.

Into the Meadow

for my father

We should have put you
where cows graze and
birds light on every limb,

where maples blaze
along an autumn fencerow
and June sends waves

of daisies, yarrow, and
buttercup, should have
tucked your bones where

you were most at home—
sun rising and setting,
grass blooming, withering—

your soul, shining
with dew, singing
its celebratory song.

My Father's Gods

after Bill Brown

My father worshipped tunnels
through Kentucky's veined earth,
followed the beam of light on his hat,
pick axe and dynamite, tamping tool
and shovel as dear as sweetheart or daughters,

worshipped camping and fishing,
swimming in Tennessee's lakes, his daughters
his congregation, a trotline and campfire
his hymnal and prayer book, we joining
a chorus he conducted wordlessly.

My father worshipped our mother,
gave us a dime for the Saturday matinee,
empty house a shrine for obeisance
to the shape and form, song and quick
laugh that was the woman he chose.

Work filled his war days at the gaseous
diffusion plant, where he pedaled a bicycle
down the mile-long building, a technician
by label, never spoke of what he saw,
what he handled, what he knew.

He worshipped his garden, soil a chalice
into which he poured the prayer of seed,
the entreaty of water and manure,
worshipped his chickens,
their feathery bodies, yellow beaks,

worshipped a final breath,
asphalt parking lot's arms open
to receive his last halleluiah.

Little Poem for a Small Word

At one year, my son
learned light,
saw it when we
switched on a lamp,
crooned the word
as the sun rose,
whispered its
liquid syllable
for headlights,
flashlight,
the brief
flicker of fireflies,
his wonder
warm as flames.

The Goldfish

The day her goldfish died
my daughter cried
three hours until her bed
was wetter that it had been
since she was two.

She had guarded the fish
against the cat, floated
fine crumbs of food
on the surface
of the amniotic fluid
where he swam,
watched his gills
open and close
in the perfect
rhythm of his living.

She was ten, life
with its cycles stalking
her own fine fluids,
her gills rehearsing
the rhythm of her life.

The Gift

Miss Carson luvs me more than yu do—
my daughter's third grade scrawl on the paper
scrap tucked in her jeans pocket. Before
the jeans drop into the washing machine
where soap swirls with tee-shirts, socks and pants,
I retrieve the lined page, press the folds flat,
smooth away wrinkles, rub fingertips
over pencil smudges, tuck the message
into my own jeans pocket. Day after
day each time my mother-anger threatens
to boil over, I touch the pocketed
slip, my daughter's silky head bent
above a page of emerging cursive,
language a tool she daily hones.

Boy after His Bath

The muscles around your shoulder blades—
those wing remnants from our reptile ancestors—
will strengthen with age, will bulge when flexed.
For now they lie smooth as the porcelain bath rim,
your hair black with wetness, a cap like a crow's
silky feathers, spinal column a ladder where nerve
ganglions climb and descend, carry messages
to arms, legs, as practiced as if you've lived forever.

Blunt fingers that know the feel of softball, fishing
pole, snake and frog, press a towel to your face.
You will not look up, will not turn away
from the task of bathing, drying, will not
acknowledge your body is a sacrament,
the ritual cleaning a daily blessing.

Making Biscuits

When my daughter measures flour,
her slender arms brush the air
like a conductor hushing the violins,
her eyes half-shut with the pleasure
of unheard chords. The blue bowl
squats on the counter. She dumps
in flour, salt, baking powder
to bake into a nest to cradle
the honey her soul craves.
Lard, like globules her body
will in its own due time grow—
cushiony bed for the children
she'll carry—drops from the spoon.
Knives in hand, she weds shortening
to flour, a union they hadn't known
they desired. Then into the bowl
a splash of buttermilk, thicker
than the blood she and I share.
Now her hands blend and mix,
flatten, roll, cut, and into the oven
where heat transforms primordial mass
into light, airy giver-of-life she'll eat,
mouth open to the gift, her body
a receptacle filling, filling.

Song to My Husband

While the sun drops low, he oils rusted bolts,
greases pipe and elbow, patience honed
by experience. Next day he will free
frozen gears, slide loose pins, clean, shine, repair.
Behind him a tractor stands in stripped glory—
fenders and hood stacked to the side, motor
like bones plucked to pistons and drive shaft.
Around his feet oily rags, bent pieces
of steel, dry leaves blown on November wind.
In the fading light, he is the only god
to be found: master of the tool box, maker
of slick parts, restorer of rusted metal,
he who brings life to what the rest of us
would bury without benediction.

One More Day

Sunlight stripes the bedroom wall, calls you
from slumber deep as wells, your beloved
lean and limber by your side, his skin the silk
you've wrapped your night in. All day you move
like liquid from stove to sink, table laden
with bread and butter, strawberries and cream.

Beyond the window cardinals hold court—
red bows in the boxwood and along maple limbs,
and in the fields crows congregate, a senate
of somber old men strutting stiff-legged,
their edicts dark memories of another life,
your world a satin surface, a day with no
appointments, a day when the phone brings no
bad news, when the mail holds only letters
from old friends. As the sun sinks behind
the mountains, you slip between smooth sheets,
a distant church bell tolls one more day's passage.

Killing Time

.... *We know*
how it will end

—Linda Pastan

As though the day
will stretch forever,
we move through
the ordinary pleasures:
sip tea in early
sunlight, slice strawberries
on a bowl of cereal,
wash the dishes
and set them to dry
on linen bleached white,
worn to a sheen
by fifty years of our
hands' touch.

We know how
it will end,
grief for one,
silence for the other,
but the days are threads,
our lives a tapestry
whose colors
soften at last
like rays of winter sun.

III. TRAVELING COMPANIONS

Sledging the Poem

for Jane Sasser

She nails
nouns and verbs
straight as floor joists,
planes simile
to metaphor,
hammers words
on the page
the way a carpenter
makes fast
a rafter
while he dreams
steepled roofs.

Symmetry

Symmetry is a stupid myth.

—J.P. Dancing Bear

Perhaps the apple has it—
two halves mirroring
one another around
an axis of sweet arsenic seeds,

or your face—hazel eyes
perfectly parted by the bridge
of your nose, twin
nostrils inhaling,

but not the maple tree—
trunk leaning toward light,
limbs like dancers bowing
and stretching each to its own music,

and not the heavens—
the Milky Way a ribbon
flung by the hand of God,
the moon winding its solitary path.

The Starry Messenger

Such a simple lesson—
a ten-year-old understands
Jupiter's moons, how they circle,
perform the dance earth
and her moon step through,
how matter yearns toward
what it sprang from. Galileo,
gazing skyward on a January evening,
saw three stars strung
on a line through Jupiter,
saw a fourth star the following evening,
their positions relative to Jupiter
shifting night by night,
his concept of stars into moons
like light sliding the length
of his telescope, exploding
into his brain, a cosmic
bang that echoes and echoes.

Everyday Poem

Every day
  I sit beneath
    the sky's
      blue tent

and I think
  how light
    is a gift—
      the one true gift

how grass
  springs forth—
    trees and mountains
      would puncture

the bright canopy
  had they
    time enough
      and strength

and I am grateful
  that grass
    though lush and fulsome
      through summer

will fade
  with fall's failing
    light, hold close
      its secret heart

how all winter
  trees will stretch
    their pale arms—
      mountains will pause.

Three Hallelujahs

i.

Hallelujah to the seasons
climbing the ridges around us,
each in its turn dressing and undressing
our landscape—timid chartreuse
into deep green into blaze of red,
orange and yellow, and then black
limbs etched sharp as memory.

ii.

Hallelujah for the blue spruce,
growing forty-plus years
in stalwart memory of my father,
its south side bare in the presence
of a sprouted maple, its spiky
tip a pyramid of green presiding
over grass and shrubs,
over land and lesser trees.

iii.

Hallelujah, we shout, for walls
that shelter us, beds that rest us,
for water to drink, a cookstove
for our vegetables, for refrigeration
and an upholstered chair
by the window, day's last rays
dying beyond the glass.
Hallelujah, for hallelujah is
an exhalation of breath, in the light-
filled space a song, the beat of a heart.

Praise

Is like the wing of a dove
fluttering in morning's light,
lifting the bird on air currents
to drift over millet fields,
wings folding in a glide,
never knowing the hunter
lies where tree's canopy
hides his camouflage,
his steely barrel.

What Is The Soul?

It could be the mockingbird
singing from the deck chair,
or the squirrel hanging
upside down on the feeder.
It could be the beagles' bay,
the coyote's cry, or something
silent as a meadow of daisies.
It could be the green snake,
a bright scribble on the drive,
or the hawk spiraling overhead,
his whistle answered by his mate,
the two a dot against an azure sky.

It could be breath flowering
in our lungs, blossoming
into the morning air, dew
moistening our feet as we cross
the clover field—the horses
whinnying for the oat sack,
their silhouette on the hilltop
the first etching of a new day.

Traveling

How long I failed to heed ... the sound
of the earth beneath my feet.

—Bill Brown

Past the garden heaped with leaves—
maple, oak for a sweet-sour soil—
beneath the apple tree, sere and gray
her withered fruit clinging through the cold

across deer tracks and close-cropped grass,
dry zinnia seeds standing for titmouse
chickadee and junco, out to compost pile
with pear peelings, spinach leaves, egg shells

trekking back as light fades and red pillars
rise above the setting sun, into the house
where soup simmers on the stove, cornbread
browns in the oven, where my footsteps wear

a forty-year groove from door to stove to table
to sink, a journey whose miles could stretch
coast to coast, span the Appalachian Trail,
a trip I had not thought to map.

Mindy at Dusk, 1919

after Dana Wildsmith

When the sun sinks behind the mountain,
Mindy is a moth folding her patterned wings.
Her skin is a lily petal in the soft darkness,
her dress a calico shadow against the gray farmhouse.
She is steady as the earth's rotation,
variable as the course of a river.
If she were a bird,
she'd be a dove.
Listen to Mindy
telling the day goodnight.
She is the whippoorwill's call,
the song the North Star hums
as it anchors the constellations.
She is moonlight on the pasture.
She is milk in the evening pail.

From a Car Window, June Afternoon

Boats speed across a green lake,
skim water's surface. Waves
trail their white lace.
Beneath tulip poplars, families
spread their lunches. Red-checkered
tablecloths whip in the breeze.
And making its way ahead of us
like a majorette strutting her stuff,
a yellow convertible beckons us gray
sedans to join life's party.

She Thinks on Hunger

She's heard it's the wolf
at the door, but she knows
there is no door, no wall,
no windows—only the landscape
like a Russian novel, tundra
reaching for miles, snow
relentless as breathing, hunger
gnawing where bone meets
sinew meets tendon, her body
a house, the wolf
stretched on the hearth.

She Pays Attention

to the work of her hands
    closes her fingers around each box,
        each bag of fruit.
The carton of eggs,
    jug of milk
        glide over the glass surface,
beep to the cash register,
    to the computer that counts inventory,
        to a screen the customer views.
The woman's rooted feet support legs,
    hips that sway oh so slightly
        to the dance of her hands—

reach, lift, swipe, set aside,
reach, lift, swipe, set aside.

For these eight hours, her arms
    forget the weight of a baby,
        press of his head against her shoulder,
smell of just-washed hair,
    wisp of sour milk breathed into her neck.
        Her heart beats with the bar-code scanner,
while its echo for nine months
    sings a steady song to other ears,
        falls asleep to the dance of other hands.
Food, shelter, clothing, another paycheck—
    each can of corn, sack of flour
        weighs like silver.

Speak These Words

Speak these words for those who cannot hear them—
the Israeli boy who crossed the street as shrapnel
burst from the suicide's car, the Palestinian girl

who rose from her bed, washed her face, repeated
her morning prayers, who went to the market for one
more day's bread, her body a magnet for the sure steel

of retaliation. For the Iraqi mother who watched
as the roof of her house grew cracks, crevices widened
into valleys, what was once solid now weapons

pounding her shoulders as she shielded her child,
ash of the old life filling their lungs. For the women
raped, the children maimed in limb and hope. For

soldiers conscripted into a life their boyhood dreams
could not imagine, pawns of old men who have never
                known
bullet's hot fire, old men who sit behind glass

safe from wavering shapes that march, make camp, stars
blotted out above tent flaps, bodies that eat, laugh,
play their card games, then rise, fall, their world

burning, burning, the old men safe from even the smoke.

Reedsong

*All day and night, music, a quiet, bright
reedsong. If it fades, we fade.*

—Rumi

And what of the mockingbird's scold,
all day his dive for the cat,
spring's bright song from the oak
silent as next December's snow?
Or the wren's churr, exhortation
to her fledglings—*fly, fly*, she calls,
then grows quiet as the empty nest?
Or the pileated's hard hammer,
maple ringing with an enduring energy
that knows nothing of fading?

Rumi, the summer reedsong on my hill
stretches with day at the solstice,
warms to its task like the baking earth
where this year's seeds swell and pop, rise
in their yeasty eagerness. If it fades,
we fade, you say—but first the wild ride,
desire the metronome that drives the hawk
in his upward spiral, cry echoing
through the long afternoon, all we know
of yearning radiant with evening light.

On the Wing

Blazing in late day sun
   vultures circle above the field
      descend and rise again
         like spray from a waterfall
           wings light as butterflies

          wheel and turn in a gyration
        that ministers to the evening
      that blesses all things
   humble, huddled, like memory
spread before the coming dark.

November Moves In

She blows open the door,
slips the cloak from her shoulders—
shades of brown disguising
threads that once shone red, gold.

Hair like frost riming the pond,
body narrow as the garden scarecrow,
she roams hall and parlor,
tosses out autumn's last vase of mums,
pulls moth-scented afghan from the closet,
peers up the fireplace chimney,
declares it too dangerous to use.

In the study, she flicks on the desk lamp,
takes out her favorite novel, *Wuthering
Heights*, settles in. She expects a pot
of tea, crisp ginger cookies,
and later a bowl of soup, wants to know
if that over-dressed hussy October
has packed her bags and fled.

Satisfied, she tries to charm us,
promises turkey, dressing and, if we
treat her right, maybe a day of sunshine
before she calls in her dark-clad kin.

Late January Letter to a
Retired Friend in Florida

Here in East Tennessee crocuses
think green while mountains wear white.
Robins flirt with spring among
yellow stalks of dry grass.
Juncoes and titmice refuse
to relinquish winter's gray.
I grow weary of woodpile,
woolen socks, cows
huddled facing into the wind.
Mud tracks mar our floors,
windows fog, frost over.

Newspapers offer the usual:
Snow-women sculpted
like Renoir's females.
Children sledding,
eyes shut, hair flying.
A pair of ducks
immobilized in a pond's ice.

The neighbors' forgotten
Christmas lights wink
through fifteen-degree nights.
Last evening, in winter's clear air,
the maple near my back door
cradled Orion among her bare limbs.
I send him to you in his icy clarity,
reminder of your friend
enduring late winter's elements,
earth's sure revolutions.

How to Spend a February Day

Never mind windowsill's dirt, corner's dust.
Go to the yellow chair by the window,
pick up the book you laid aside last night
when the baby cried. Brew a cup of tea,
dark leaves giving up moisture to ease
winter's dry crackle. Feel the heft of mug,
how clay, water, heat meld into vessel.
Test liquid on your tongue. Pay obeisance
to generations who withstood wind, weather
without furnace, insulation, thermo-pane.
Think earthworms, ladybugs, soil's dark regions,
how dormancy seeps through each cell. And your
life, how joyous sunlight on a face that
knew winter wind, icy chill of January.

Pain

My old friend is back,
arrived with his luggage
prepared for a lengthy stay.
He refuses the guest room,
climbs into bed with me,
kneads my joints
with fingers of knuckled bones.
We sleep spooned together,
lovers who ache
for one another's bodies,
his neediness the pulse
that measures my night,
our union as sure as
a long marriage.

He will rise with me
at daybreak, stay by my side
through tea and toast,
laundry and sweeping,
his arm encircling my back
while I feed the birds,
gather the last green tomatoes.
Faithful as my old dog,
sure as the slipping of day into night,
he will not abandon me,
has trothed his love,
a groom more foreboding
than childhood's nightmares.

Old Age

A train moving through the night,
it has huffed into our station.
The passengers—pain, sorrow, grief
and all their dark-robed relatives—lean out
the windows, wave their bony hands, beckon us closer.

We settle among them, play a hand
of gin rummy, munch chicken legs
from their picnic baskets, cast sidelong
glances toward the caboose door.
Even now it sluices open
and we recognize the conductor
making his way up the aisle, the punch
for our tickets hanging from his belt loop,
our destination the final stop.

Poppies

Do you see a thread in the bloody silk
of the poppy?

—Pablo Neruda

I know the poppy, scraggly stems breaking earth
in mid-April, leaves like moth-eaten lace.

And then the blossoms—crepe paper cups
of pistil and stamen, food for May's butterflies.

And yes, bloody silks falling atop the dining
table, yellow pollen peppering the linens.

The flowers are childhood's dreams, perfect petals
like pictures on a calendar, the promise of summer

and long leisurely days, the lie that the world
slows, that whatever we want will come. Poppies

in a field, brown with July heat, only the oval
of a seed head ripe for picking, opium for some

other mind, our own pleasure fled. Do you see
a thread in the bloody silk of the poppy, Neruda

asks, a seam in the world where childhood is stitched
in yesterdays, sewn into the fabric of day

following night following day, a seam that lies
flat in our memory, pulled tight with each breath.

Traveling Companions

after Lisel Mueller

i. How I Would Pack for Happiness

Happiness would take along
her yellow dress, the one patterned
with butterflies and daisies,
she would take sandals to show off
her painted toenails, throw
a hot-pink bikini into the bag
and sunglasses large enough
to block out all glare.

ii. How I Would Pack for Beauty

An armful of roses she'll carry,
and her make-up bag—mascara,
vermillion lipstick, silky face
powder—an elegant evening
dress studded with sequins
like the glittering heavens.

iii. How I Would Pack for Health

She'll need walking shoes,
a handful of vitamins, an apple
rosy as sunrise, a bottle of spring
water, salad greens fresh
from the garden, will power
for the climb, and a soft pillow
to guarantee deep sleep.

iv. How I Would Pack for Regret

Nothing but gray clothing—
long skirt to reach her ankles,
a veil to hide her face,
lace-trimmed handkerchief
she'll twist and twist.

v. How I Would Pack for the Past

Corsets that clinch from behind,
bustles, feet bound for tiny shoes,
and the wardrobe you never
want to see again—Nehru
jackets, bell-bottom jeans,
and garments made of polyester.

vi. How I Would Pack for the Future

She'll need swiftness, shoes
that skim the surface of moon
and planets, a rocket on her back
maneuvering the heavens,
imagination her only map,
loneliness her private companion.

vii. How I Would Pack for Death

I would not pack for Death.
He carries his own valise,
black as night, its contents
his secret, only the rattle
of his bones to tell us he
follows just behind,
each halting step drawing
him closer and closer.

Spite

Turned the picnic into a wake,
sent the birds into early migration,
closed the petals on the daylily,
came calling on a summer afternoon
when we wanted only to rock in the shade.

She curled up on the glider,
took all the pillows for herself,
salted the pie we had cooling
on the windowsill, melted the ice
meant for the tea. She recounted
the tales our cousin was spreading
about our sister, whispered where
Grandpa had hidden his whiskey.
She said she meant no harm,
told us these things for our own good,
if we'd help her a bit—refuse to forget
who stole our marble when we were four,
remember all the fusses and fights—
she might spend her entire vacation with us.

Winter Rides the Mountains

after reading Charles Wright

Winter rides the mountains, stalks the valleys.
How colder than ever the backyard.
Dogs huddle in leaf piles,
daylight brings her paint brushes,
gray and black for this day,
here and there a patch of white.

Winter days I drift with the wind,
aimless as a scrap of paper
blown into the ell of the house.
Tomorrow will be cold, the next day colder still.
Of what use—a seventy-year-old woman,
a frozen January morning?

Beneath it all, seeds sleep,
earthworms burrow, lady bugs
hang out in clusters.
Above the silence, breathe,
breathe, step softly on earth's bed.

From the Pulpit: For the Minister at My Memorial Service

Say here lies someone
who was ordinary as maple trees,
who went out and came in
all the days of her life
glorying in the repetitive,
hoping for the unexpected,
who loved a summer storm
rippling the pond's surface,
who sought refuge in the garden,
weeds and vegetables numbered
as companions, one to test her soul,
the other a gift that deceived
with joy, wearied with its exuberance.
Say she had a spiritual side
hidden from the overly religious,
her prayers a dirty floor
and a stiff, soapy brush,
her hymns the daily laundry
lifting its arms to the wind.
Say she is grateful for earth's
brief sharing, less than a wave
against the endless yaw of ages,
the wearing down of mountains,
rush and roil of oceans.
Say finally that she died
praising the power of breath,
the endless stretch
of conscious into unconscious,
of making into being
into merging
into rising.

May

Han-Shan wakes delighted

—George Scarbrough

and so do I—
yesterday at the garden's edge,
I paused before the tumble
of roses climbing the fence,
the wild dance of pea vines
handing their partners along the rows,
watched the bluebird fly
in and out of his box

and I passed by without entering,
the sun's yellow bowl filled
with all the day needed.

Self-Portrait

I am child of mother, father,
sisters, child of my own children
who held my hand through our joint
growing up, child of my husband
who taught me turn, taught me
open heart, giving spirit.

In winter weather, I am gray limbs
stretched toward a grayer sky,
I am hearth and fire, stones warmed
to the touch. My husband splits logs,
hauls them to the back door,
their burning my fierce desire.

All year the land cradles me,
black earth split into spring's furrows,
summer's vines climbing hand over hand
along the fence, fall's melons ripened
into husks of orange or green, shells
that hide sweet secrets to fill winter meals.

Though the years ahead are few, they sing
as the sirens, lure me toward landfall where
a multitude of voices have only just begun
their blending, their notes ascending.

About the Author

Connie Jordan Green lives on a farm in East Tennessee with her husband and two cats and two dogs. Her weekly column for the *Loudon County News Herald* is in its 36th year. She writes stories for young people, poetry, and novels. The novels received various awards: *The War at Home* was placed on the ALA List of Best Books for Young Adults, both books were selected by the New York City Library as books for the Teen Age, *The War at Home* was nominated to the 1991-92 Volunteer State Book Award Master List, and *Emmy* was selected as a Notable 1992 Children's Trade Book in the Field of Social Studies. Her poetry has appeared in numerous publications and has won awards. She has two chapbooks from Finishing Line Press, *Slow Children Playing* and *Regret Comes to Tea*. She was the recipient of a Lifetime Achievement Award from the East Tennessee Hall of Fame for Writers. She teaches for the Oak Ridge Institute for Continued Learning (ORICL), and leads writing workshops. She and her husband have three children and seven grandchildren.

Our Mission

The mission of Brick Road Poetry Press is to publish and promote poetry that entertains, amuses, edifies, and surprises a wide audience of appreciative readers. We are not qualified to judge who deserves to be published, so we concentrate on publishing what we enjoy. Our preference is for poetry geared toward dramatizing the human experience in language rich with sensory image and metaphor, recognizing that poetry can be, at one and the same time, both familiar as the perspiration of daily labor and as outrageous as a carnival sideshow.

Also Available from Brick Road Poetry Press

www.brickroadpoetrypress.com

Etch and Blur by Jamie Thomas

Water-Rites by Ann E. Michael

Bad Behavior by Michael Steffen

Tracing the Lines by Susanna Lang

Rising to the Rim by Carol Tyx

Treading Water with God by Veronica Badowski

Rich Man's Son by Ron Self

Just Drive by Robert Cooperman

The Alp at the End of My Street by Gary Leising

The Word in Edgewise by Sean M. Conrey

BRICK ROAD
POETRY PRESS

Also Available from Brick Road Poetry Press

www.brickroadpoetrypress.com

Dancing on the Rim by Clela Reed

Possible Crocodiles by Barry Marks

Pain Diary by Joseph D. Reich

Otherness by M. Ayodele Heath

Drunken Robins by David Oates

Damnatio Memoriae by Michael Meyerhofer

Lotus Buffet by Rupert Fike

The Melancholy MBA by Richard Donnelly

Two-Star General by Grey Held

Chosen by Toni Thomas

About the Prize

The Brick Road Poetry Prize, established in 2010, is awarded annually for the best book-length poetry manuscript. Entries are accepted August 1st through November 1st. The winner receives $1000 and publication. For details on our preferences and the complete submission guidelines, please visit our website at www.brickroadpoetrypress.com.